Number Textbook

Peter Patilla
Ann Montague-Smith
Paul Broadbent

Addison Wesley Longman Limited

Edinburgh Gate, Harlow, Essex, CM20 2JE, England

First published 1996

© Addison Wesley Longman Limited 1996

Designed and typeset by Gecko Limited
Illustrations by Gecko Ltd, Katey Farrell, Madeleine Hardy, Tania Hurt-Newton, Peter Richardson

ISBN 0582 28836 3

The Publisher's policy is to use paper manufactured from sustainable forests.

Produced by Longman Asia Limited, Hong Kong

CONTENTS

Number facts

Begin at the **START** and answer the first question.
Follow the line to the next question.
Keep a note of the letters that you pass on the way.
Answer all the questions until you reach the **FINISH**.
What does the message say?

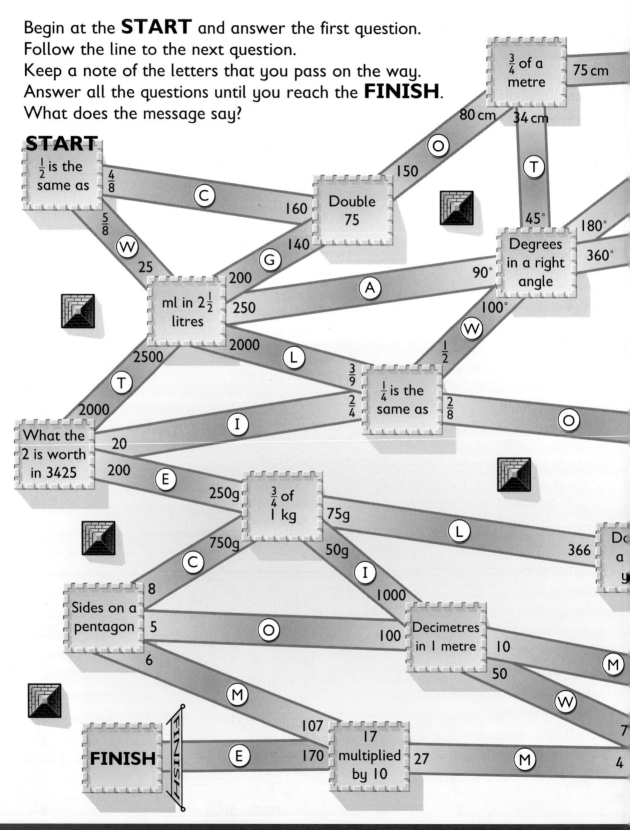

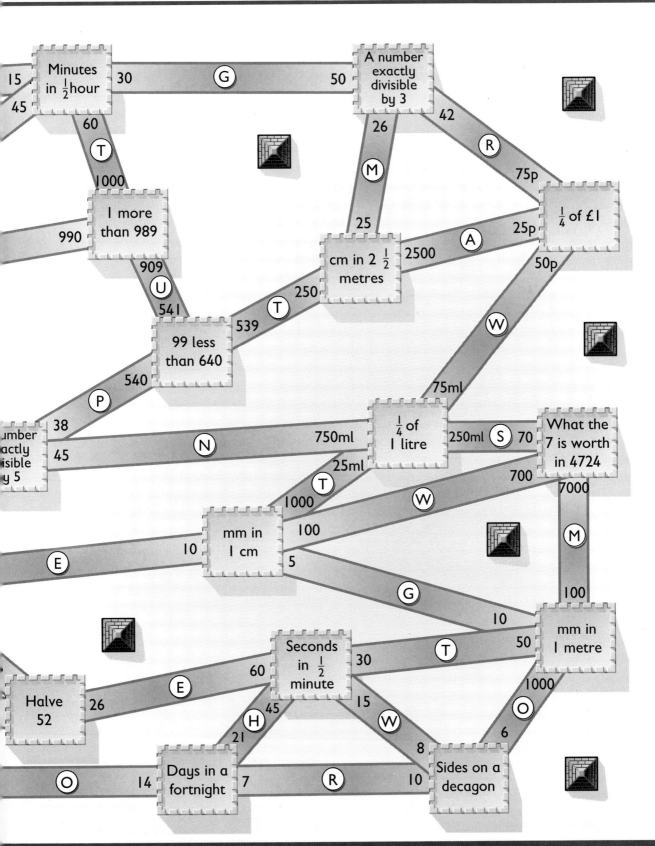

Abacus numbers

Throughout history, different types of counting aids have been used.
The Romans placed pebbles in columns.

Did You Know?

The Romans called these pebbles **calculi**.
This is how the word calculate came to be used.

The Romans usually added a bar across the abacus.
A pebble placed above the bar stood for 5.

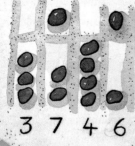

3 7 4 6

A Write the number shown on each Roman abacus.

1.  2. 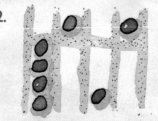 3.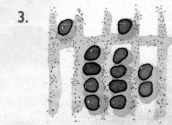

B Write the number shown on each frame abacus.

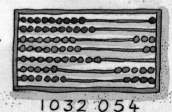

1032054

1. 2. 3.

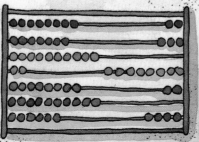

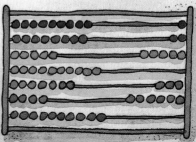

Unit 1

Teacher's Handbook page 35

Soroban numbers

The Roman abacus was adapted and used in China during the twelfth century. It was also used in Japan, where it was called a **soroban**.

The soroban had enough rods to record at least two four-digit numbers side-by-side.

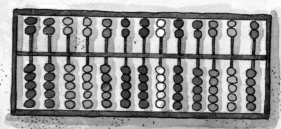

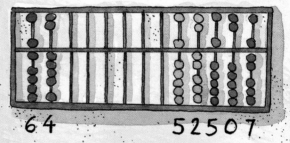

64   52507

 A   Write the two numbers that are shown on each soroban.

1.
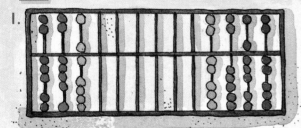

2.
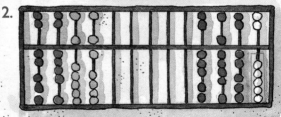

3.
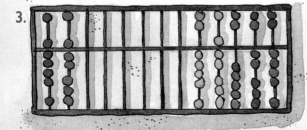

4.

Did You Know?

The soroban is still widely used in the East. Skilled users can often work faster than a calculator!

Roman numerals

A line drawn over Roman numerals multiplies them by 1000.

$\overline{\text{CCL}}$ = 250 000 $\overline{\text{DC}}$ = 600 000

(250 × 1000)   (600 × 1000)

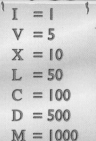

I	= 1
V	= 5
X	= 10
L	= 50
C	= 100
D	= 500
M	= 1000

A Write the numbers these Roman numerals represent.

1. $\overline{\text{LXI}}$ 2. $\overline{\text{VII}}$ 3. $\overline{\text{CLX}}$ 4. $\overline{\text{CXX}}$ 5. $\overline{\text{DLX}}$

B Multiply each of these numbers by 100.

1. 104   2. 350   3. 700   4. 1574   5. 3640

C Divide each of these numbers by 100.

1. 3700   2. 40 000   3. 32 000   4. 560 000   5. 100 000

D Divide each of these numbers by 1000.

1. 48 000   2. 3 600 000   3. 401 000   4. 880 000   5. 1 000 000

Challenge

Write each of these numbers in Roman numerals.

57 000 = $\overline{\text{LVII}}$

1. 30 000   2. 99 000   3. 124 000

4. 500 000   5. 304 000

The letter K is sometimes used to stand for thousands.

The cost of the car is £75 000.

A Write these numbers in full.

1.
> New computer
> has 64K memory

2.
> 65K attend
> football match

3.
> Pop star makes
> £500K on tour

4.
> 17K children enter
> maths competiton

5.
> Lost library books:
> 5K go missing each
> year

6.
> Salaries rise
> to 48K

B Mille or milli at the beginning of a word usually means thousand.
Copy and complete the following.

1. Millennium = ☐ years

2. ☐ millimetres = 1 metre

3. ☐ millilitres = 1 litre

4. One million = ☐ thousands

C Write the numbers that are linked to the following 'starters'.
1. Centi   2. Deca or deci   3. Penta   4. Hexa   5. Tri

Did You Know?

The mile was a Roman unit of length. It was 1000 double paces of a Roman soldier. The word 'mile' comes from the Latin 'mille passus', which means 'one thousand paces'.

A Calculius has mixed up the labels from these chests of money.
Can you match each label with the right chest?

1.    2.    3.    4.

96 coins   254 coins   750 coins   1,000 coins

Now estimate how many coins are in each of these chests.

5.    6.   7.    8.    9.

B Round the number of coins in each chest to the nearest 100.

1.    2.    3.    4.    5.

794   1,409   3,251   4,749   7,850

C Round the number of coins in each chest to the nearest 1000.

1.   2.    3.    4.    5.

7,246   9,842   5,500   11,299   21,816

A This map shows the population of some English counties.

Answer the following questions.

1. Write the approximate population of each county to the nearest 10 000.
2. Which county has a population closest to half a million?
3. Which county has a population closest to that of Buckinghamshire?

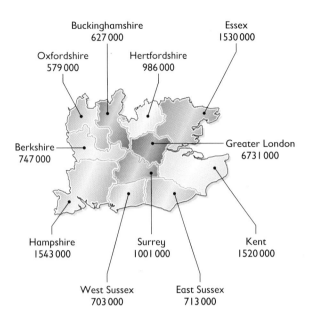

Buckinghamshire 627 000
Essex 1530 000
Oxfordshire 579 000
Hertfordshire 986 000
Berkshire 747 000
Greater London 6731 000
Hampshire 1543 000
Surrey 1001 000
Kent 1520 000
West Sussex 703 000
East Sussex 713 000

B This table shows the approximate population of some British cities. Answer the following questions.

1. Which is the largest city?
2. Which cities have a population of less than 300 000?
3. Which city has a population closest to 400 000?
4. Which cities have a population over 500 000?
5. List the cities in order of population, starting with the largest.

	Population		Population
Sheffield	528 000	Glasgow	716 000
Edinburgh	438 000	Bradford	464 000
Wakefield	312 000	Bristol	378 000
London	6731 000	Liverpool	470 000
Wigan	307 000	Wolverhampton	294 000
Cardiff	284 000	Doncaster	292 000
Coventry	306 000	Sunderland	296 000
Belfast	297 00	Stockport	291 000
Birmingham	994 000	Leeds	710 000
		Manchester	446 000

Negative numbers

Look at the timeline below.

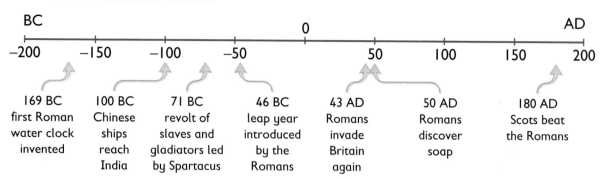

 A How many years passed between:

1. The Romans' first water clock and the discovery of soap?
2. The Chinese reaching India and the first leap year?
3. The slaves' revolt and the Scottish victory?

Challenge

Do you know the meaning of BC and AD?

Can you work out how many leap years there have been?

B Write the differences between the numbers in the following pairs. Drawing a number line might help.

1. 7, −4
2. −3, 8
3. −10, 12
4. −8, −2
5. 15, −15

C 1. Enter 4 − − = 0 on your calculator.

Enter 1 2 = = = = = Write and continue the pattern for ten numbers.

2. Try different patterns like these.

3 − − = 0   5 − − = 0   8 − − = 0

then   then   then

1 2 = = =   1 2 = = =   1 2 = = =

World facts

The diagram shows some of the high and low points on the Earth.

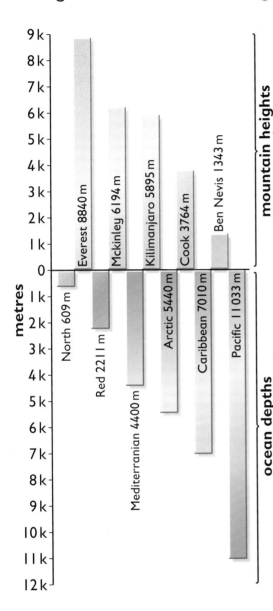

A Write the difference between:
1. The top of Mount Everest and top of Ben Nevis;
2. The top of Mount McKinley and the bottom of the Arctic Ocean;
3. The top of Cook Island and the bottom of the Mediterranean;
4. The top of Kilimanjaro and the bottom of the Pacific Ocean;
5. The bottom of the North Sea and the bottom of the Caribbean Sea.

B The table shows the temperature on the planets:

Venus	480° C
Mercury	350° C
Mars	−23° C
Jupiter	−150° C
Saturn	−180° C
Uranus	−210° C
Neptune	−220° C
Pluto	−230° C

Find the temperature difference between:
1. Mars and Mercury;
2. Venus and Pluto;
3. Jupiter and Neptune;
4. Saturn and Uranus.

Did You Know **?**

Mauna Kea in Hawaii is 1356 m taller than Mount Everest but only 4205 m is above sea level.

Decimus always stands between any two numbers.

A Write six numbers that Decimus and any two of these numbers can make.
Write the numbers in order, starting with the smallest.

B Use the number line to help you to write each of these decimals to the nearest whole number:

1. 3.7   2. 2.4   3. 4.5   4. 5.1   5. 2.3   6. 3.6

C Write what you would need to add to each decimal to round it to the next whole number.
For example, 6.7 is rounded up to 7 by adding 0.3.

1. 3.4   2. 7.8   3. 6.5   4. 8.2   5. 1.9   6. 4.1

D Copy the following pairs of numbers and write >, < or = between each pair of numbers to make each statement true.

1. $2\frac{1}{2}$ ☐ 2.6

2. $5\frac{1}{2}$ ☐ 5.4

3. $4\frac{1}{2}$ ☐ 4.9

4. $3\frac{1}{2}$ ☐ 3.5

5. $2\frac{1}{2}$ ☐ 2.5

6. $5\frac{1}{2}$ ☐ 5.3

A Estimate the position of each coin on the number line.

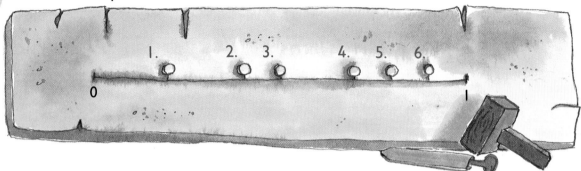

 B Write which decimal number the green shield stands for.

C Write these fractions as decimals.

1. $1\frac{3}{10}$

2. $2\frac{7}{10}$

3. $4\frac{9}{10}$

4. $3\frac{1}{2}$

5. $1\frac{1}{5}$

6. $2\frac{2}{5}$

INVESTIGATE

Find pairs of numbers that have 1.4 as their halfway position?
Can the pair be whole numbers?

1.1   1.4   1.7

Tens   Units   Tenths   Hundredths

A   Write the value of 7 in each number.

1. | 1 | · | 3 | 7 |

2. | 4 | · | 7 | 2 |

3. | 7 | · | 5 | 8 |

4. | 7 | 9 | · | 1 | 4 |

5. | 7 | 2 | 3 | · | 4 |

6. | 1 | 6 | 3 | · | 7 |

7. | 5 | 7 | 2 | · | 8 |

8. | 4 | 0 | 9 | · | 7 |

9. | 7 | 1 | 6 | · | 4 |

B   Write these numbers in order, starting with the smallest.

1.   1.52   1.5   1.2

2.   3.4   3.29   3.42

3.   2.04   2.4   2.41

4.   8.42   8.24   8.4

5.   4.55   4.5   4.05

6.   5.6   5.63   5.36

C   Write each decimal to the nearest whole number.

1. 4.2

2. 2.56

3. 2.64

4. 1.53

5. 2.05

6. 1.09

This table shows the cost of sending parcels.

Weight up to	Speedy Mail	Snail Mail
500 g	86p	65p
600 g	£1.05	95p
700 g	£1.25	£1.05
750 g	£1.35	£1.10
800 g	£1.45	Not allowed over 750 g
900 g	£1.60	
1000 g	£1.85	
Each extra 250 g (or part) 55p		

 A Write what it would cost to send each of these parcels by Speedy Mail.

1.   2.   3.   4.

B Write which parcel can be sent by Snail Mail and how much it would cost.

Challenge

Can you work out how much this parcel weighs?
Explain your answer.

The balloon race

THE GREAT EUROPEAN BALLOON RACE

Air Distance (km)

	Berlin	Edinburgh	London	Madrid	Paris
Edinburgh	1497				
London	934	608			
Madrid	1871	1864	1264		
Paris	880	949	341	1054	
Rome	1182	2034	1434	1365	1108

A Write the distance of each stage of the race.
1. Paris to Madrid
2. Madrid to Rome
3. Rome to Berlin
4. Berlin to Edinburgh
5. Edinburgh to London
6. London to Paris

B Travelling by the shortest route, what is the total distance from Paris to Madrid, then to Rome?

C Calculate these distances.

1.	1162 km	2.	1079 km	3.	1083 km	4.	1063 km
	+ 1429 km		+ 1391 km		+ 1428 km		+ 1469 km

D Total these.
1. 3079 + 6219
2. 4381 + 3739
3. 1098 + 6212
4. 3944 + 1865

A This chart shows the points scored for two stages of the balloon race.

Balloon name	Madrid	Rome	Total
Voyager	6821 points	3109 points	9930 points
Pilgrim's Progress	6790 points	3127 points	
Sky Trek	6781 points	3009 points	
Cloud Cruiser	6135 points	2998 points	
The Wanderer	5979 points	3017 points	

Copy the chart and fill in the missing totals.

B Find the totals for these.

1. 5819 +3046
2. 5792 +2968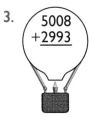
3. 5008 +2993

4. 4812 +2875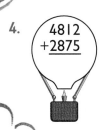
5. 4299 +2684
6. 3958 +2876
7. 3847 +2763

C Four pairs of numbers add up to a total of 5000.
  1. Write the pairs of numbers.
  2. Now find four pairs of numbers that add up to 8000.

2792	2614	3281	4212
4183	1175	3817	1943
3825	2208	5179	2386
1719	3788	6057	2821

Subtraction

This hot air balloon holds 285 kg.
The crew drop 68 kg of ballast
to increase their height.
The weight in the balloon
is now 217 kg.

$$\begin{array}{r} 285\,\text{kg} \\ -\ \ 68\,\text{kg} \\ \hline 217\,\text{kg} \\ \hline \end{array}$$

A Answer these sums.

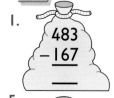

1.
```
  483
– 167
─────
```

2.
```
  672
– 314
─────
```

3.
```
  748
– 129
─────
```

4.
```
  514
– 306
─────
```

5.
```
  684
– 395
─────
```

6.
```
  821
– 599
─────
```

7.
```
  948
– 269
─────
```

8.
```
  461
– 395
─────
```

B 'Counting on' can be used to find the difference between two numbers.
The difference between 327 and 839 is 512.

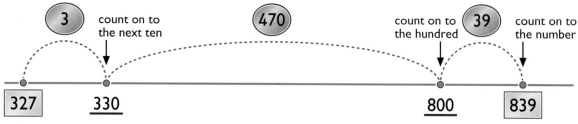

Count on to find these differences.

1. 872 – 568
2. 643 – 279
3. 571 – 387
4. 434 – 156
5. 583 – 329
6. 454 – 296

Differences

 A Each balloon can take 3500 units of fuel.
These dials show how much fuel has been used.
Write how much is left.

1. Voyager

2. Pilgrim's Progress

3. Sky Trek

4. Cloud Cruiser

5. The Wanderer

 B Find the difference between these pairs of numbers.

1. 5831
   7214

2. 6490
   3527

3. 9800
   8104

4. 7211
   5396

5. 8204
   6799

6. 7901
   9480

 C Find the difference in height between Mont Blanc and each of the other mountains in the Alps.

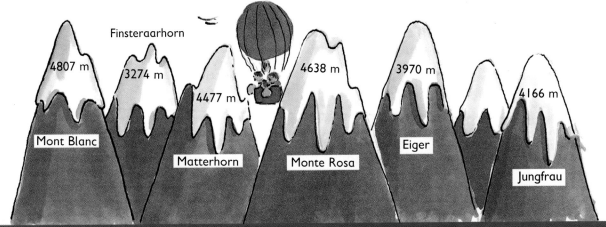

Finsteraarhorn

4807 m
3274 m
4477 m
4638 m
3970 m
4166 m

Mont Blanc
Matterhorn
Monte Rosa
Eiger
Jungfrau

A Copy these sums and fill in the missing digits.

1.
```
  3 8 □ 4
+ □ 1 6 □
---------
  6 0 3 7
```

2.
```
  □ 9 2 □
+ 3 □ 1 9
---------
  8 6 4 7
```

3.
```
    4 □ 1 □
+   □ 1 □ 3
-----------
1 0 0 0 4
```

4.
```
  □ 8 4 4
+ 5 □ 6 □
---------
1 2 8 □ 9
```

5.
```
  □ 3 3 □
- 2 □ 7 8
---------
  4 1 6 1
```

6.
```
  4 □ 8 □
- □ 9 1 5
---------
  1 9 6 9
```

7.
```
  8 4 □ 5
- 2 8 7 □
---------
  5 □ 5 9
```

8.
```
  □ 0 6 0
- 1 1 9 □
---------
  1 □ 6 7
```

B Work out the answers to the following calculations.
Use the code breaker to change the last digit
of each answer to a letter.
Rearrange the letters to find the name of a capital city.

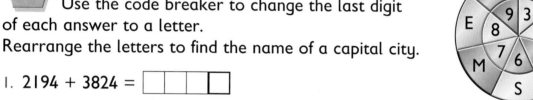

1. 2194 + 3824 = ☐☐☐☐

2. 4732 − 1493 = ☐☐☐☐

3. 6892 − 4835 = ☐☐☐☐

4. 3921 + 4726 = ☐☐☐☐

5. 8249 + 1067 = ☐☐☐☐

6. 6931 + 2138 = ☐☐☐☐

7. 4961 − 3856 = ☐☐☐☐

8. 8439 − 1525 = ☐☐☐☐

9. 3876 − 2193 = ☐☐☐☐

INVESTIGATE

Choose four digits.
Rearrange them to make the largest number.   7521
Now make the smallest number.   1257
Find the difference between the two numbers.   6264
Make the largest number with those digits.   6642
Now make the smallest number.   2466
Find the difference.   4176
Continue.
When does the chain end?
Investigate different four-digit numbers.

Unit 2   Adding and subtracting money

$£\ 12 \cdot 42 + 6 \cdot 81 = 19 \cdot 23$

$£\ 73 \cdot 21 - 14 \cdot 19 = 59 \cdot 02$

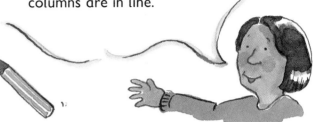

If you add and subtract money in this way, make sure the columns are in line.

A   Answer these sums.

1. £4.27 + £19.31
2. £18.06 + £23.40
3. £31.99 + £6.47
4. £12.39 – £6.05
5. £29.45 – £14.82
6. £67.59 – £9.16

B   Find the total cost for each of the shopping lists.

Watches £4.85

Remote control car

Car £28.40

Remote control car

Models £3.49

All pens £1.37

Doll house £21.99

Kites £5.69

Radios £17.95

Lamps £12.75

Torch £2.99

Pencil pots £1.20

1.
Torch
Radio
Lamp

2.
Kite
Watch
Pen

3.
Doll house
Pencil pot
Model

4.
Remote control car
Radio
Kite

How much change from £20 you would get from each of these items?

5.
6.
7.
8.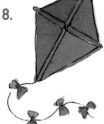

Estimating

Did You Know ?

The heptathlon has seven events and the decathlon has ten events. High jump and long jump are two of the events. Can you find out the names of the others?

A Work out each athlete's score.

6. Who has the most points?

B One thousand people can sit in each section of this athletics stadium when it is full.
Estimate how many people are in each section.

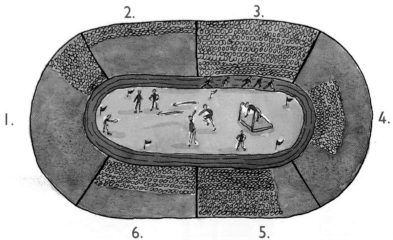

7. Find the approximate total of the crowd.

Rounding thousands

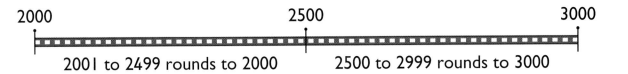

2000   2500   3000

2001 to 2499 rounds to 2000   2500 to 2999 rounds to 3000

A   Round these numbers to the nearest thousand.

1. 1382	2. 4609	3. 1099	4. 6701	5. 9178
6. 3921	7. 8489	8. 7504	9. 5014	10. 6582

B

Queens Park Athletic Club	
Month	Attendance
April	1466
May	3792
June	4209
July	5894
August	4503
September	4099
October	3184

Kings Avenue Athletic Club	
Month	Attendance
April	1899
May	2920
June	5039
July	4672
August	4712
September	3872
October	3502

1. Round each figure to the nearest thousand. Draw a chart for each of the clubs. Write the rounded figures on the charts.
2. Which club has the highest approximate attendance?
3. Write the actual total attendances of each club to the nearest thousand.

Rounding can help you to find the approximate
answers to check your work.
Rounding 2276 + 4821 gives 2000 + 5000.
The approximate answer is 7000.
What is the exact answer?

A   Write the approximate answer and then the exact answer to
these sums.

1. 8016 + 1327
2. 6930 + 2871
3. 5214 + 1918
4. 6924 + 1842
5. 7314 − 3018
6. 7297 − 2841
7. 3848 − 1919
8. 4931 − 2853

B   Write the correct answer for each of these sums.
Choose from the numbers in the brackets.
Rounding the numbers will help you.

1. 2149 + 3824 + 1927 =   (6400, 7900, 9200)

2. 3842 + 1271 + 2904 =   (6217, 7117, 8017)

3. 8131 − 4928 =   (3203, 5230, 2403)

4. 7894 − 1046 =   (5948, 6848, 7984)

C   Write the approximate
answers to these sums.

4279 − 677
round
4300 − 700 → approximate answer → 3600

1. 8251 + 467 + 724
2. 5244 + 3712 + 499
3. 5914 + 336 + 1128
4. 4620 − 769
5. 11 304 − 9654
6. 17 858 − 965

Mental methods

To add 98:

first add 100 then

subtract 2

73 + 98 = 171

To add 297:

first add 300 then

subtract 3

426 + 297 = 723

A Copy and complete this table.

To add	First add	Then subtract
99	100	
197		
399		
296		
498		

B Work out these sums in your head. Then write down your answers.

1. 323 + 99   2. 107 + 198
3. 84 + 297   4. 72 + 97
5. 288 + 199   6. 346 + 396

To subtract 197:

first subtract 200

then add 3

To subtract 99:

first subtract 100

then add 1

284 − 99 = 185

422 − 197 = 225

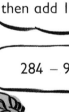

C Copy and complete this table.

To subtract	First subtract	Then add
198	200	
297		
98		
396		
495		

D Work out these sums in your head. Then write down your answers.

1. 242 − 98   2. 437 − 199
3. 654 − 397   4. 341 − 298
5. 528 − 299   6. 723 − 196

Using brackets

Brackets are used to show which part of a number problem to work out first.

$$(6 \times 4) - 3 = 21$$
$$24 - 3 = 21$$

$$(15 - 8) - (3 + 2) = 2$$
$$7 - 5 = 2$$

$$6 \times (4 - 3) = 6$$
$$6 \times 1 = 6$$

 A Copy and complete these sums.

1. $(3 \times 8) - 4 = \square$

2. $5 \times (8 - 2) = \square$

3. $(2 \times 9) + 7 = \square$

4. $5 \times (2 - 1) = \square$

5. $(7 \times 3) + (4 \times 2) = \square$

6. $(4 + 3) - (8 - 7) = \square$

7. $(4 \times 9) - 7 = \square$

8. $(3 \times 2) + (8 - 2) = \square$

B Copy these sums, using one pair of brackets in each to make the equation true.

1. $18 - 5 + 3 = 10$

2. $4 \times 3 + 6 = 18$

3. $27 - 6 + 2 = 23$

4. $8 - 6 \times 0 = 0$

5. $8 + 2 \times 5 = 18$

6. $7 + 2 \times 2 = 18$

C Copy these sums, using brackets in each to make the equation true.

1. $2 \times 8 - 5 \times 3 = 1$

2. $18 - 3 + 4 - 2 = 17$

3. $3 \times 4 + 5 \times 2 = 22$

4. $8 - 5 \times 6 + 3 = 27$

5. $9 - 7 + 4 - 2 = 4$

6. $4 + 3 \times 8 - 2 = 42$

 INVESTIGATE

Use the digits $\boxed{1}$ $\boxed{2}$ $\boxed{3}$ $\boxed{4}$, brackets and $\times \div + -$.
Make up sums which have answers from 1 to 12.
Use digits only once in each sum.

$$(3 \times 2) - (4 + 1) = 1$$

A number which reads the same backwards as forwards is called a palindrome.

Numbers like: 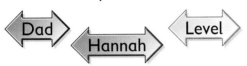 are palindromes.

Some words are palindromes too.

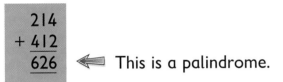

A Choose any three-digit number. Reverse the digits and add the two numbers.

```
  214
+ 412
  626
```
⇐ This is a palindrome.

Choose another number.

```
  253
+ 352
  605
```
⇐ This is not a palindrome.

If the answer is not a palindrome, reverse it and add the two numbers.

```
  605
+ 506
 1111
```
⇐ This is a palindrome.

Did You Know?

Ferdinand De Lesseps, the designer of the Panama Canal, had this written on his gravestone:

A MAN A PLAN A CANAL PANAMA

Read it backwards.

ESTIGATE

Investigate other numbers. Do you always get a palindrome?

B Are palindromic numbers always multiples of 11?

Multiplication

 A Write the digits 0 to 9 on small squares of paper.
Find a home for each digit.
Write out the sums.

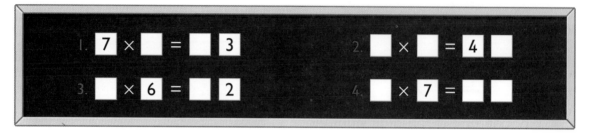

1. 7 × ☐ = ☐ 3   2. ☐ × ☐ = 4 ☐
3. ☐ × 6 = ☐ 2   4. ☐ × 7 = ☐ ☐

B Copy these sums and fill in the missing numbers.

○ × ○ ⟹ 24	○ × ○ ⟹ 36	○ × ○ ⟹ 8
× ×	× ×	× ×
○ × ○ ⟹ 56	○ × ○ ⟹ 30	○ × ○ ⟹ 18
21 64	24 45	24 6

C Copy and complete these sums.

1. 9 × ☐ = 36   2. 7 × 7 = ☐   3. ☐ × 4 = 32   4. 7 × 6 = ☐
5. 8 × 8 = ☐   6. ☐ × 6 = 54   7. 6 × ☐ = 36   8. 8 × 7 = ☐

D Each of these sums has several possible solutions.
Write three different solutions for each problem.

1. ☐ × ☐ = 24   2. ☐ × ☐ = 18   3. ☐ × ☐ = 36

A Write your answers to the following questions.

1. It is six weeks to bonfire night.
How many days is this?

Six fireworks are packed into each box.

November						
S	S	M	T	W	T	F
		1	2	3	4	(5)
6	7	8	9	10	11	12
13	14	15	16	17	18	19

2. How many boxes are needed for 48 fireworks?
3. How many fireworks in nine boxes?
4. Laura saved £3 a month for fireworks.
How many months did it take to save £24?
5. There were 72 pieces in a slab of bonfire toffee.
The slab was nine pieces long.
How many pieces wide was the slab of toffee?

B Complete the sums and write the answers in words.
Read the letters in the red boxes to find the names of two fireworks.

$6 \times 6 =$ t h i r t y s i x $4 \times 5 =$ _ _ _ _ _ _

$7 \times 9 =$ _ _ _ _ _ _ _ _ _ $6 \times 4 =$ _ _ _ _ _ _ _ _ _ _

$9 \times 9 =$ _ _ _ _ _ _ _ _ $4 \times 8 =$ _ _ _ _ _ _ _ _ _

$6 \times 8 =$ _ _ _ _ _ _ _ _ _ $6 \times 10 =$ _ _ _ _ _

$6 \times 7 =$ _ _ _ _ _ _ _ $9 \times 2 =$ _ _ _ _ _ _ _ _

$3 \times 4 =$ _ _ _ _ _ _ $9 \times 8 =$ _ _ _ _ _ _ _ _ _ _

$8 \times 8 =$ _ _ _ _ _ _ _ _ _ $8 \times 10 =$ _ _ _ _ _ _ _

$4 \times 7 =$ _ _ _ _ _ _ _ _ _ _ _ $7 \times 5 =$ _ _ _ _ _ _ _ _ _ _

$8 \times 3 =$ _ _ _ _ _ _ _ _ _ _ _ $3 \times 9 =$ _ _ _ _ _ _ _ _ _ _ _

                                            $2 \times 6 =$ _ _ _ _ _ _

At the garden centre

A Write sums to answer these questions.

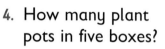

1. What would six packets of seed cost?

2. What would eight bulbs cost?

3. How many seedlings in 17 trays?

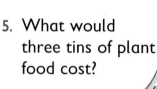

4. How many plant pots in five boxes?

5. What would three tins of plant food cost?

6. What would four pairs of gloves cost?

B Check the instructions and answer the questions.

Use 1 scoop for each 25 litres of water

Spread 25g on each square metre

LAWN SEED

POND CLEAR

1. How many scoops for 600 litres of water?

2. How many grams to cover 9 square metres?

Add 5 millilitres to each litre of water

Spread 7 caps full over each square metre

LIQUID COMPOST

3. How many millilitres in 25 litres of water?

WEED KILLER

4. How many caps full to cover 35 square metres?

C Answer these sums.

1. 54 × 6   2. 79 × 5   3. 35 × 8   4. 46 × 9
5. 87 × 3   6. 95 × 2   7. 82 × 7   8. 63 × 5

Challenge

□□
× □
‾‾‾‾‾

‾‾‾‾‾

Choose three digits:

2 4 5 7 8 9

Make the largest number.
Make the smallest number.

A Write sums to answer these questions.

1. There are 96 plants altogether. How many are in each box?

2. 84 flowers were sold in bunches of six. How many bunches is this?

3. One third of the plants are red. How many plants are red?

54 PLANTS

4. There are equal numbers of three types of plants in the tray. How many of each type?

48 mixed plants

5. One fifth of the plants have been planted. How many is this?

80 PLANTS

6. One quarter of the plants are ready for planting. How many is this?

64 plants

B If the seeds are shared equally between the seed trays, how many will be in each tray? Write the sums and answers.

1. SEEDS 72
2. SEEDS 75
3. SEEDS 96
4. SEEDS 98
5. SEEDS 78
6. SEEDS 92

C Answer these sums.

1. 4)98
2. 3)92
3. 6)83
4. 8)96
5. 3)87
6. 5)86
7. 9)98
8. 7)87

Taking stock

A Lisa is checking the stock in the tuck shop.
Copy the stock lists below and fill in the totals.

1.

Number of packets in each box	Number of boxes	Total number of packets
30 Fizzers	6	
40 Choccos	5	
80 Crunchers	7	
60 Fruitees	8	
50 Sparkles	3	

2.

Number of packets in each box	Number of boxes	Total number of packets
50 Nutty bars	4	
20 Caramels	9	
90 Chewies	3	
70 Suckers	7	
40 Toffees	8	

B Lisa works out answers like this:
Use Lisa's method to write your answers to these.

263	UNITS	$3 \times 6 = 18$
$\times\ 6$	TENS	$60 \times 6 = 360$
	HUNDREDS	$200 \times 6 = \underline{1200}$
	TOTAL	$\underline{1578}$

1. 424
   $\times\ 3$
   ___

2. 614
   $\times\ 5$
   ___

3. 195
   $\times\ 8$
   ___

4. 237
   $\times\ 4$
   ___

5. 316
   $\times\ 2$
   ___

C Choose your own way to answer these.

1. 506
   $\times\ 6$
   ___

2. 825
   $\times\ 7$
   ___

3. 496
   $\times\ 5$
   ___

4. 721
   $\times\ 4$
   ___

5. 419
   $\times\ 3$
   ___

D David is checking the stock in the stationery cupboard.

1. How many pens altogether?

2. How many exercise books altogether?

3. How many rulers altogether?

4. What would 350 pencils cost?

5p each

5. What would 180 pencil sharpeners cost?

9p each

6. What would 240 erasers cost?

3p each

Multiplying prices

A Daniel has worked out how much six rolls of wallpaper will cost.

$$\begin{array}{r} £4.46 \\ \times\ 6 \\ \hline £26.76 \end{array}$$

Write the cost of these items.

1. six light bulbs £1.55

2. four paint brushes £2.58

3. eight rollers  £2.99

4. seven coat hooks £3.08 each

5. nine bags of nails  £2.34

6. six packets of wallpaper paste £4.52

B Write the cost of the following items.

1. 500 washers
2. 300 nails
3. 200 screws
4. 900 carpet tacks
5. 700 bolts
6. 250 picture hooks

Washers	*£5.45 per 100*
Nails	*£6.95 per 100*
Screws	*£5.99 per 100*
Carpet tacks	*£7.35 per 100*
Bolts	*£7.65 per 100*
Picture hooks	*£2.99 per 50*

C Copy and complete these bills.

1.
4 plants @ £1.36 =
2 books @ £0.99 =
3 pots @ £2.65 =
           Total =

2.
6 canes @ £1.29 =
5 cactii @ £3.99 =
4 fish @ £2.35 =
           Total =

3.
3 nets @ £4.75 =
9 pkt seeds @ £1.49 =
8 bags compost @ £4.99 =
           Total =

D Complete these bills.

1.
 pinks £2.45
 asters £2.99

2.
 roses £4.50
 wall flower £2.35

2 × ☐ + 3 × ☐ = £13.33   3 × ☐ + 4 × ☐ = £22.90

Buying furniture

A Write the cost of:
1. 50 chairs
2. 30 bedside tables
3. 40 stools
4. 20 lamps
5. 60 rugs
6. 30 mirrors

B Find the answers to these.
1. 90 × 30   2. 60 × 80   3. 50 × 50   4. 70 × 60
5. 40 × 90   6. 70 × 40   7. 80 × 70   8. 30 × 80

C Ian is buying some office furniture.
He finds the cost of buying 38 typing chairs like this:

$$£26 \atop \times 30 \over £780$$ $$£26 \atop \times 8 \over £208$$ So £26 × 38 = 780
                                                     208
                                                     £988

Use Ian's method to find the cost of these:
1. 28 chairs
2. 34 desks
3. 42 cupboards
4. 29 tables
5. 56 filing cabinets
6. 37 bookcases

D Use your own method to calculate the answers to these sums.

1. 27 × 34   2. 56 × 25   3. 42 × 21   4. 54 × 19
5. 26 × 26   6. 31 × 28   7. 58 × 17   8. 23 × 46

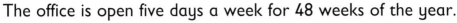

A The office is open five days a week for 48 weeks of the year.

1. Each day 125 catalogues are posted.
How many are sent in a year?

2. Stamps cost 25p each.
What is the weekly postage cost for the catalogues?

3. The catalogues cost 27p each to print.
What is the yearly cost for printing catalogues?

B Find the cost of buying the following office supplies.

Box of labels	Ring binders	Pencils (50)	Pens (25)	Rolls of tape (10)	Bulldog clips (each)
£1.24	£2.07	64p	78p	93p	3p

1. 25 ring binders
2. 36 boxes of labels
3. 800 pencils
4. 300 pens
5. 200 rolls of tape
6. 86 bulldog clips

C It costs £27.75 per day to put a full-page advertisement in a newspaper.
A half-page advertisement costs £15.65.

1. Calculate the cost of placing a full-page advertisement for 26 days.
2. What would 48 half-page adverts cost?
3. Find the cost of twelve full-page and eighteen half-page advertisements.

D Calculate each person's wage.
The hourly rates are double for working on a Saturday or Sunday.

Mohammed £4.74 per hour	hours
Monday	6
Tuesday	6
Wednesday	3
Thursday	6
Friday	8
Saturday	6
Sunday	$4\frac{1}{2}$

Sandra £4.25 per hour	hours
Monday	6
Tuesday	-
Wednesday	-
Thursday	6
Friday	8
Saturday	8
Sunday	8

Francis £3.80 per hour	hours
Monday	3
Tuesday	6
Wednesday	6
Thursday	3
Friday	3
Saturday	$4\frac{1}{2}$
Sunday	$4\frac{1}{2}$

Ways of dividing

 A Answer the following sums.
1. 58 ÷ 4   2. 87 ÷ 3   3. 124 ÷ 3   4. 207 ÷ 5
5. 326 ÷ 6   6. 256 ÷ 8   7. 593 ÷ 6   8. 603 ÷ 9

 B

 Not very good at dividing by 6? Try halving both numbers.

$$6\overline{)318}$$

$$3\overline{)159}$$

Try halving both numbers in these problems.
1. $6\overline{)516}$ 2. $6\overline{)928}$ 3. $8\overline{)642}$ 4. $8\overline{)936}$

5. $14\overline{)336}$ 6. $14\overline{)658}$ 7. $18\overline{)414}$ 8. $18\overline{)810}$

 C

Sometimes you can halve the numbers again and again.

Write your answers to these divisions.
1. $8\overline{)472}$ 2. $12\overline{)684}$ 3. $16\overline{)464}$ 4. $16\overline{)528}$

 D Divide each of these numbers by 10 and write the remainder.

1. 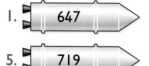 647   2. 328   3. 809   4. 572

5. 719   6. 999   7. 625   8. 452

 E

Try doubling both numbers. Check if it changes the answers.

$$5\overline{)135}$$

$$10\overline{)270}$$

Use the doubling method to answer these.
1. $5\overline{)175}$ 2. $5\overline{)245}$ 3. $5\overline{)365}$ 4. $5\overline{)415}$

A Divide 2519 by each number from 1 to 10 in turn.
What do you notice about the remainders?

B Divide each number by 8 to find the remainders.
Use the code to change the
remainders into letters.
Rearrange the letters to find the
names of fruit.

Code	0	1	2	3	4	5	6	7
Breaker	B	N	O	A	R	G	E	P

1. 375 275 158 212

2. 311 500 451 405 582

3. 524 675 393 437 758 618

4. 769 427 552 179 233 371

 C Calculators do not give remainders.
They turn the remainder into a decimal.

```
   64 r 4
5 )324
```

Write the remainder and decimal remainder for these sums.

1. 4)322
2. 3)571
3. 5)337
4. 4)721
5. 5)806
6. 2)921

Challenge

Use a calculator to help you to answer these.

1. 6)□□□□ → 3 5 8
2. □□)1778 → 127
3. 8)461 → 57 r. □
4. 5)□□□ → 2 6 r. 3

Approximating

An equals sign with a bump on top means 'nearly equal' or 'approximately'.

A Write the approximate answers to these divisions.

$460 \div 5 \simeq 90$

1. $650 \div 8 \simeq$
2. $310 \div 4 \simeq$
3. $390 \div 5 \simeq$
4. $550 \div 9 \simeq$
5. $470 \div 6 \simeq$
6. $570 \div 7 \simeq$
7. $190 \div 3 \simeq$
8. $410 \div 8 \simeq$

B

round
$281 \div 4 \implies 280 \div 4$

round
$659 \div 9 \implies 660 \div 9$

round
$236 \div 6 \implies 240 \div 6$

Round these numbers, then write the approximate answers.

1. $284 \div 4 \simeq$
2. $423 \div 6 \simeq$
3. $358 \div 7 \simeq$
4. $439 \div 6 \simeq$
5. $719 \div 9 \simeq$
6. $325 \div 5 \simeq$
7. $168 \div 3 \simeq$
8. $596 \div 8 \simeq$

C Solve these equations. Estimate then check.

1. $207 \div \boxed{} = 23$
2. $152 \div \boxed{} = 38$
3. $520 \div \boxed{} = 65$
4. $328 \div \boxed{} = 41$
5. $135 \div \boxed{} = 27$
6. $171 \div \boxed{} = 19$
7. $512 \div \boxed{} = 64$
8. $608 \div \boxed{} = 76$

D Each of these numbers is exactly divisible by 9. The last digit is hidden.

Write the numbers.

1. 26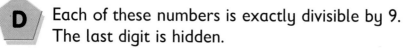
2. 58
3. 41
4. 34
5. 64

Map codes

 A Use the digits of each answer as coordinates. For example:

> 288 ÷ 8 = 36   On the map go three along then six up.

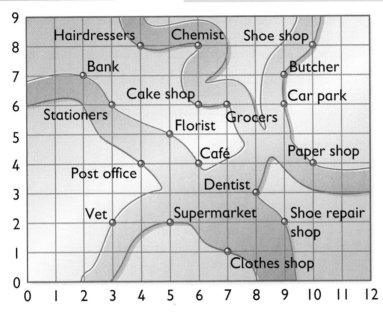

Prue visited the stationer on her trip to town.
Make a list of other places visited in town using the same method.

1. 544 ÷ 8 _____
2. 608 ÷ 8 _____
3. 864 ÷ 9 _____
4. 581 ÷ 7 _____
5. 828 ÷ 9 _____
6. 312 ÷ 6 _____
7. 384 ÷ 6 _____
8. 396 ÷ 9 _____
9. 189 ÷ 7 _____
10. 528 ÷ 8 _____

**ESTIGATE**

Enter a three-digit number on a calculator.
Repeat the digits to make a six-digit number.

Divide by 7 ➤ Then divide by 11 ➤ Finally divide by 13 ➤

Write what you notice.
Repeat for other six-digit numbers made this way and write what happens.

Fractions of shapes

 A Copy these shapes on to squared paper.
Draw a straight line to cut each area in half.

 1. 2. 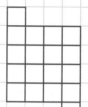 3. 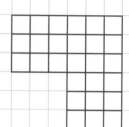 4.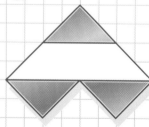

Now try the same with these.

5.  6.  7.

B Estimate the fraction which is coloured on these badges.

1. 2. 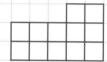 3.

4. 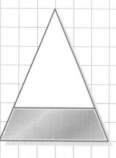 5. 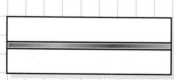 6.

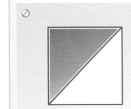

$\frac{1}{2} = \frac{2}{4}$

$\frac{1}{2}$ and $\frac{2}{4}$ are equivalent fractions.

This means that they have the same value.

A Copy and complete the statement under each diagram.

1.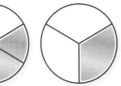

$\frac{2}{6} = \frac{\square}{3}$

2.

$\frac{3}{4} = \frac{\square}{8}$

3.

$\frac{4}{10} = \frac{\square}{5}$

4.

$\frac{\square}{8} = \frac{1}{2}$

5.

$\frac{\square}{3} = \frac{\square}{9}$

6.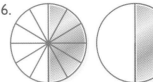

$\frac{\square}{12} = \frac{\square}{\square}$

B Write two equivalent fractions for each of these diagrams.

1.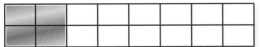

2.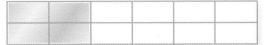

C On squared paper, show each of these equivalent fractions as a diagram.

1. $\frac{2}{3} = \frac{4}{6}$ 2. $\frac{1}{2} = \frac{4}{8}$ 3. $\frac{3}{5} = \frac{6}{10}$

A Copy these statements, adding one of these symbols > < or = to make each statement true.

1. $\frac{1}{2}$ ☐ $\frac{2}{4}$
2. $\frac{3}{8}$ ☐ $\frac{3}{4}$
3. $\frac{2}{3}$ ☐ $\frac{5}{6}$
4. $\frac{2}{6}$ ☐ $\frac{1}{3}$

5. $\frac{4}{6}$ ☐ $\frac{2}{3}$
6. $\frac{1}{4}$ ☐ $\frac{1}{8}$
7. $\frac{3}{4}$ ☐ $\frac{5}{8}$
8. $\frac{7}{8}$ ☐ $\frac{3}{4}$

B Copy these statements, adding one of these symbols > < or = to make each statement true.

1. $\frac{1}{3}$ ☐ $\frac{2}{4}$
2. $\frac{3}{6}$ ☐ $\frac{4}{8}$
3. $\frac{7}{8}$ ☐ $\frac{6}{6}$
4. $\frac{1}{4}$ ☐ $\frac{1}{3}$

C Copy the table, writing each fraction in the correct column.

Less than $\frac{1}{2}$	More than $\frac{1}{2}$

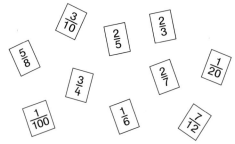

$\frac{3}{10}$ $\frac{2}{5}$ $\frac{2}{3}$ $\frac{5}{8}$ $\frac{3}{4}$ $\frac{2}{7}$ $\frac{1}{20}$ $\frac{1}{100}$ $\frac{1}{6}$ $\frac{7}{12}$

D Write the statement below in four different ways, writing the missing numbers so that it is true each time.

$$\frac{1}{\square} = \frac{2}{\square} = \frac{3}{\square}$$

Write what you notice about any patterns.

Unit 4 Cube fractions

Use interlocking cubes for these activities.

 A This is quarter of a shape.
Make six different models. What could the whole shape look like?

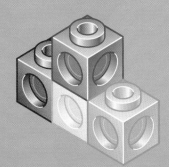

 B
Make a cuboid using 16 cubes.

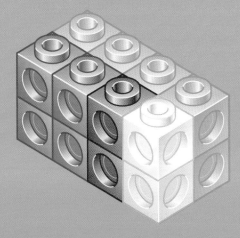

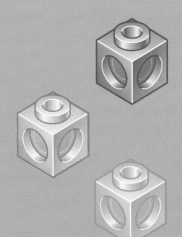

Use different colours to make up the cuboid.
Make: $\frac{1}{2}$ green, $\frac{1}{4}$ blue, $\frac{1}{8}$ red, $\frac{1}{16}$ yellow, $\frac{1}{16}$ white.

Challenge

Make different cuboids, using different colours, to show:

1. $\frac{1}{2}$ $\frac{1}{3}$ $\frac{1}{6}$
2. $\frac{1}{2}$ $\frac{1}{4}$ $\frac{1}{6}$ $\frac{1}{12}$

Bird table

Class 5 kept a tally chart of the birds visiting their bird table during one day.

Bird	Tally	Total
Sparrow	ⅢⅠ ⅢⅠ ⅠⅠ	
Starling	ⅢⅠ ⅠⅠⅠⅠ	
Pigeon	ⅢⅠ Ⅰ	
Bluetit	Ⅰ	
Blackbird	ⅢⅠ	
Robin	ⅠⅠⅠ	
Total number of birds		

A Answer the following questions.
 1. How many times did each type of bird visit the bird table?
2. What was the total number of birds?

What type of bird made up:
3. $\frac{1}{4}$ of the total?
4. $\frac{1}{3}$ of the total?
5. $\frac{1}{6}$ of the total?
6. $\frac{1}{12}$ of the total?

B Write the answers to the following fractions.
 1. $\frac{1}{6}$ of 30 2. $\frac{1}{4}$ of 24 3. $\frac{1}{8}$ of 56 4. $\frac{1}{5}$ of 40
 5. $\frac{1}{3}$ of 24 6. $\frac{1}{10}$ of 90 7. $\frac{1}{6}$ of 36 8. $\frac{1}{7}$ of 7

C On one day, 48 birds visited the bird table.

$\frac{1}{2}$ were sparrows	$\frac{1}{6}$ were robins
$\frac{1}{4}$ were starlings	$\frac{1}{12}$ were pigeons

Draw a chart to show the number of birds visiting the bird table.

Unit 4 Birds

A Write the answers to the following fractions.
1. $\frac{1}{4}$ of 8
2. $\frac{1}{5}$ of 10
3. $\frac{1}{3}$ of 9
4. $\frac{3}{4}$ of 8
5. $\frac{4}{5}$ of 10
6. $\frac{2}{3}$ of 9

B Write the answers to the following fractions.
1. $\frac{2}{3}$ of 12
2. $\frac{3}{5}$ of 20
3. $\frac{5}{6}$ of 18
4. $\frac{3}{10}$ of 20
5. $\frac{3}{4}$ of 36
6. $\frac{7}{10}$ of 30
7. $\frac{2}{5}$ of 15
8. $\frac{3}{8}$ of 16

C These numbers show how many peanuts there are in each container. Write $\frac{3}{4}$ of each of these numbers.

1.  16
2.  24
3.  40
4.  20
5.  32

Challenge

This bird has eaten $\frac{1}{3}$ of the nuts.
How many nuts were put out?

Investigating fractions

 A Each of these shapes covers $\frac{1}{2}$ the geoboard.

On spotty paper, draw six more ways of halving the geoboard.

 B Each of these shapes covers $\frac{1}{3}$ of the geoboard.

On spotty paper, draw six more ways of covering $\frac{1}{3}$ of the geoboard.

INVESTIGATE

What fractions can you show on a 3 × 3 geoboard?

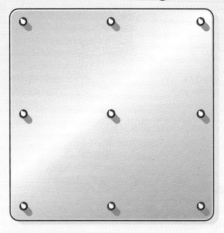

Each of these patterns has been drawn on a 4 x 4 grid.

 A $\frac{1}{2}$ of each grid is coloured.

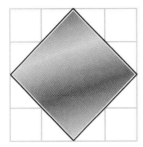 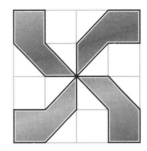

On squared paper, make four patterns of your own by colouring half the grid.

 B $\frac{1}{4}$ of each grid is coloured.

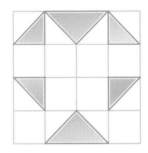 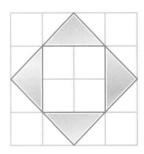

On squared paper, make four patterns of your own by colouring quarter of the grid.

 C $\frac{5}{8}$ of each grid is coloured.

On squared paper, make four patterns of your own by colouring five-eighths of the grid.

**ESTIGATE**

Choose a fraction.
Make different fraction patterns on a grid.

Welby Sports Centre

This is a plan of Welby Sports Centre.

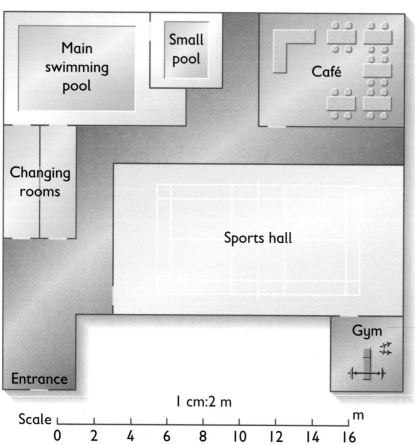

Scale   1 cm:2 m

0   2   4   6   8   10   12   14   16   m

Admission Prices

	Adults	Juniors (under 12)
Badminton	£3.80	£2.25
Table tennis	£1.20	£0.90
Basketball	£3.20	£2.40
Gym	£3.10	£1.80
Swimming	£1.60	£0.80
Spectators	£0.30	£0.20

Pool Timetable

7.00–8.00 am	Early Birds
10.00–11.30 am	Senior citizens (main pool)
10.00–11.30 am	Parent and toddler (small pool)
12.30–6.00 pm	Public swimming
6.00–7.00 pm	Welby swimming club
7.30–9.00 pm	Adults' session

Use the floor plan, price list and timetable on page 50 to answer these questions.

 A Find the area of each of these.

1. Sports hall
2. Changing rooms
3. Main swimming pool
4. Café
5. Gym
6. The whole sports centre

B Find the perimeter of each of these.

1. Changing rooms
2. Small pool
3. Café
4. Sports hall
5. Gym
6. The whole sports centre

 C Find the admission charge for each of these groups.

1.
Two adults
and two juniors
swimming.

2.
One adult and
three juniors
swimming and
one adult spectating.

3.
Four adults and six
juniors playing
basketball.

 D Answer the following questions.
1. How long is the senior citizens' swimming session?
2. How much longer is the adults' swimming session than the early birds?
3. How long is the public swimming session?
4. For how long is the pool closed during the day?

Welby Swimming Club

Current number
of members: 48
Cost per week: £3
Hours: 6 – 7.00 pm
           Monday – Friday

Lengths swam: 14 October
Aaron ——→ 32 lengths
Mark ——→ 29 lengths
Lucy ——→ 27 lengths
Paula ——→ 24 lengths

Best times – 80 metres
Boys
    Aaron Powell – 1 min. 24 secs.
    Jamie Parr – 1 min. 26 secs.
    Sammy Lee – 1 min. 31 secs.
    Mark Watkins – 1 min. 35 secs.
Girls
    Rachel Smith – 1 min. 32 secs.
    Paula Rogers – 1 min. 38 secs.
    Laura Norton – 1 min. 44 secs.
    Lucy Parr – 1 min. 47 secs.

A   Answer these questions.

1. How many metres did Aaron, Mark, Lucy and Paula swim altogether on October 14th?
2. Laura swims $\frac{3}{4}$ of the distance of Aaron. How far does she swim?
3. Rachel swims $\frac{2}{3}$ of the distance of Paula. How far does she swim?
4. Sammy swims 880 m. How many lengths does he swim?
5. How much does each daily session cost?
6. How long did it take Mark Watkins to swim 80 m?
7. How much longer does Sammy Lee take to swim 80 m than Aaron Powell?
8. Two-thirds of the club members are girls. How many boys are there in the swimming club?

BASKETBALL LEAGUE TABLE

Positions	Played	Won	Lost	Points scored	Points against	Total
1 Manchester Giants	29	25	4	2934	2369	50
2 Thames Valley Tigers	28	25	3	2632	2164	50
3 Worthing Bears	28	23	5	2608	2367	46
4 Guildford Kings	27	17	10	2352	2171	34
5 Birmingham Bullets	26	16	10	2213	2086	32
6 Derby Bucks	28	15	13	2492	2458	30
7 London Towers	29	15	14	2450	2577	30
8 Leicester Riders	27	13	14	2199	2195	26
9 Sunderland Scorpions	30	11	19	2633	2791	22
10 Chester Jets	30	10	20	2430	2541	20
11 Doncaster Panthers	27	6	19	2111	2301	16
12 Hemel Royals	27	3	24	2263	2689	6
13 Oldham Celtics	28	1	27	2135	2743	2

A   Answer the following questions.

    1. How many games have the Doncaster Panthers won?

2. How many points have the London Towers scored?
3. Which team has had the fewest points scored against them?
4. Which teams have scored more points than they have had scored against them?
5. Which team has won $\frac{1}{9}$ of their games?
6. Which team has won $\frac{1}{3}$ of their games?
7. Which team has $\frac{1}{5}$ of the total of the London Towers?
8. Which team has scored the least points?

B   The Manchester Giants have scored 2934 points.
     They have had 2369 points scored against them.
The points difference is $2943 - 2369 = 565$.
Write down the points difference for the other teams.

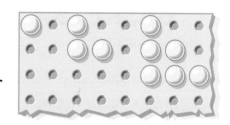

A Use a pegboard and pegs to make a pattern of triangles like this.

1. Write the number of pegs in each pattern.
2. Write what you notice about these triangular numbers.

Predict the next number in the pattern and check whether you were correct.

B Use interlocking cubes to make an increasing pattern of shapes like this.

Record the pattern on squared paper.
Write about number patterns you notice.

 INVESTIGATE

Investigate this growing pattern.
Write about the patterns you notice.

Unit 5 Square and triangular numbers

 A On squared paper, colour a pattern of L shapes like this:

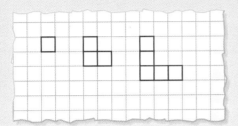

Continue the pattern, making larger L shapes.
Cut out the L shapes and fit them together to make squares.
Write what you notice about the pattern.

 B Cut out these shapes from squared paper:

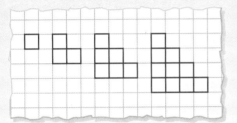

Cut out the next two shapes in the sequence.
- Count the number of squares in each shape. Write what these numbers are called.
- Arrange the shapes in pairs to make squares and stick them onto paper.
- Write about the patterns you notice.

 C Copy these diagrams.

1. Venn Diagram

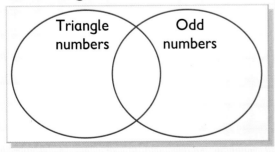

2. Carroll Diagram

	Square numbers	Not square numbers
Odd numbers		
Not odd numbers		

Write the numbers 1 to 30 in each diagram.

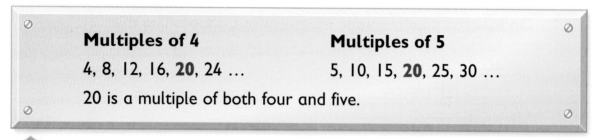

Multiples of 4

4, 8, 12, 16, **20**, 24 ...

Multiples of 5

5, 10, 15, **20**, 25, 30 ...

20 is a multiple of both four and five.

A

1. List the first ten multiples of 3.
2. List the first ten multiples of 4.
3. Write the numbers which are multiples of 3 and 4.

B Write three numbers which would fit in the shaded part of each Venn Diagram.

1.

Multiples of 6	Multiples of 8

2.

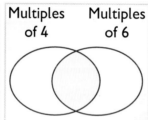

Multiples of 4	Multiples of 6

3.

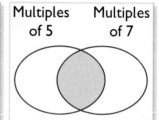

Multiples of 5	Multiples of 7

4.

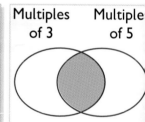

Multiples of 3	Multiple of 5

C

1. Find the numbers on the code wall which are multiples of 4.
Write the matching letters.
Rearrange the letters to make the name of a city.

S	D	F	L	I	L
27	61	35	8	40	9
C	B	D	F	E	N
7	4	36	70	54	24
I	R	E	U	D	A
49	21	18	12	42	14

2. Do the same with the multiples of 6, 7 and 9.

Factors

The factors of 12 1, 2, 3, 4, 6, 12	**The factors of 15** 1, 3, 5, 15

A Copy and complete these arrow diagrams.

➡ = is a factor of

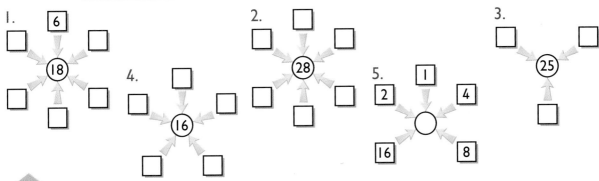

B Draw arrow diagrams to show factors of:

1. 20   2. 24   3. 21   4 30

INVESTIGATE

On squared paper draw all the rectangles that can be made from 36 squares.

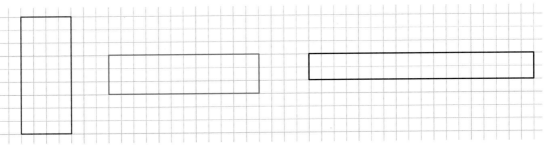

Investigate making rectangles from different numbers of squares.

Coordinates

This is a map of Coombe Point and Castle Island.
The castle is at coordinates (15, 4).

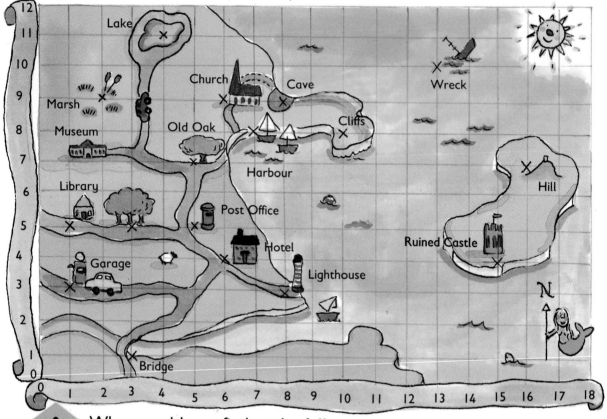

A What would you find at the following points?

1. (3,1)   2. (8,3)   3. (4,11)   4. (10,8)   5. (16,7)

B Write the coordinates of the following places.

1. The wreck   2. The marsh   3. The old oak
4. The hotel   5. The garage

C There is treasure hidden somewhere on the map.

Join coordinates (3,5) and (7,9).
Join coordinates (7,5) and (3,9).
The treasure is hidden where the lines cross.
Write the coordinates of the treasure.

Challenge

Draw your own map with coordinates.

Bury some treasure and leave clues to find it.

Unit 5   Shapes and coordinates

These coordinates have been joined
with straight lines to make a triangle.

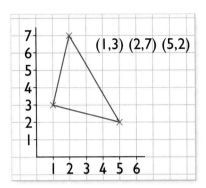

(1,3) (2,7) (5,2)

A   Copy the grid and plot the following coordinates.
Join each set of coordinates with a coloured line to make a triangle.

1. (2,1) (6,1) (4,5)
2. (2,6) (6,3) (2,3)
3. (3,4) (5,7) (6,1)

B   Draw these quadrilaterals on grids and name them.

1. (1,1) (2,3) (5,3) (4,1)
2. (1,4) (1,7) (6,7) (6,4)
3. (2,3) (2,6) (5,6) (5,3)
4. (3,7) (1,5) (3,1) (5,5)

Challenge

Design a star on squared paper.
Write down the coordinates for
a friend to follow to draw the
star.

A Copy the tables of results.
Write the numbers which come out of each of these machines.
Write one thing you notice about each pattern.

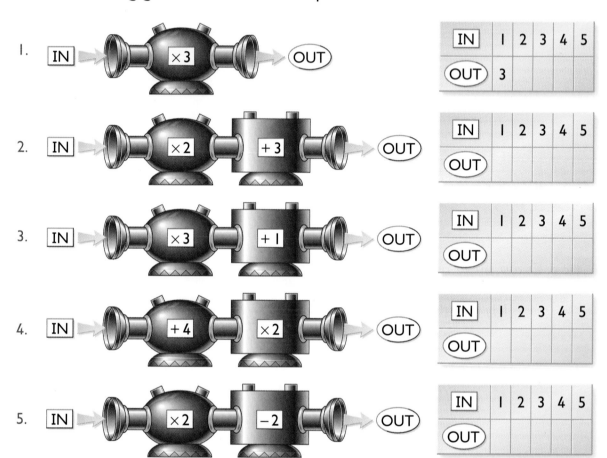

1.

IN	1	2	3	4	5
OUT	3				

2.

IN	1	2	3	4	5
OUT					

3.

IN	1	2	3	4	5
OUT					

4.

IN	1	2	3	4	5
OUT					

5.

IN	1	2	3	4	5
OUT					

B Copy and complete the following diagrams.

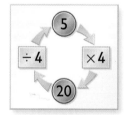

1.

2.

3.

4.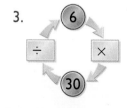

Unit 5   More function machines

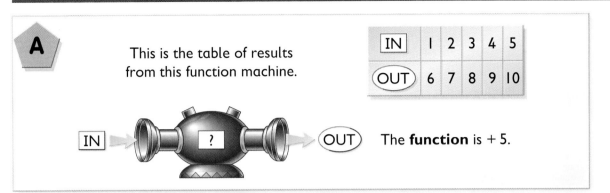

Draw function machines for these tables of results.

1.

2.

IN	1	2	3	4	5
OUT	7	8	9	10	11

3.

4.

IN	1	2	3	4	5
OUT	10	20	30	40	50

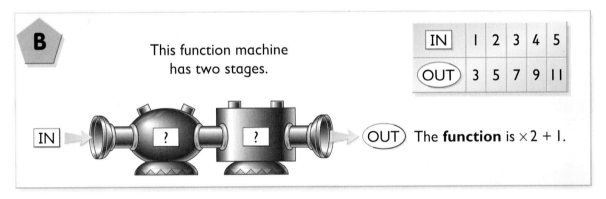

Draw function machines for these tables of results.

1.
IN	1	2	3	4	5
OUT	4	6	8	10	12

2.
IN	1	2	3	4	5
OUT	2	5	8	11	14

3.
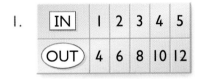

4.
IN	1	2	3	4	5
OUT	9	19	29	39	49

Stick patterns

A Use counters and sticks.
Complete each pattern and continue for another three rows.
Copy the table of results and write what you notice about each pattern.

1.

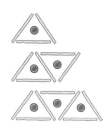

⬤	╱
1	3
2	5

2.

⬤	╱
0	1
1	2
2	3

3.

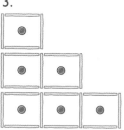

⬤	╱
1	4
2	7

4.

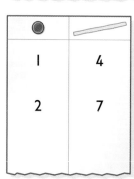

⬤	╱
3	3
4	5
5	

INVESTIGATE

How many counters ?

How many sticks ?

How many squares ?

Continue the sequence and write about the patterns.

Challenge

Make up your own stick patterns.

62 Number sequences   Counters, sticks   Teacher's Handbook page 85

A Use a calculator to work out these sums.
Write about the patterns you find.
Do the patterns continue?

1.

$143 \times 7 \times 1$
$143 \times 7 \times 2$
$143 \times 7 \times 3$
$143 \times 7 \times 4$

2.

6×7
66×67
666×667
6666×6667

3.

$1 \times 9 + 2$
$12 \times 9 + 3$
$123 \times 9 + 4$
$1234 \times 9 + 5$

4.

$1 \times 8 + 1$
$12 \times 8 + 2$
$123 \times 8 + 3$
$1234 \times 8 + 4$

5.

37×3
37×33
37×333
37×3333

6.

91×44
91×444
91×4444
91×44444

Challenge

Make up your own calculator patterns.

A Draw this Venn Diagram and write the numbers 1 to 24 on your diagram.

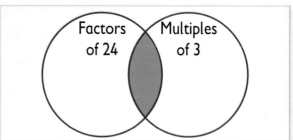

 B Copy this diagram.
Write the numbers 1 to 16 on your diagram.

	Multiple of 2	Factor of 30	Factor of 12	Odd
Between 3–16				
Factor of 18				
Less than 9				
Greater than 11				

C Copy this diagram.
The triangles show the differences between adjacent numbers.
Write the numbers 1 to 9 on small pieces of paper. Arrange them on your diagram so that all of the differences shown are correct. Copy the numbers into the squares.

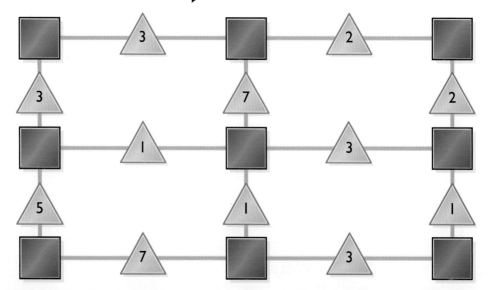

A Put ten counters on the petals of this flower. Counters must not be placed in spaces that touch.

B Play this game with a partner.
Rules

- Take turns to put a counter in a space on this pattern.
- Counters cannot be placed in spaces that touch.
- The player to place the final counter wins.
- Play three games.

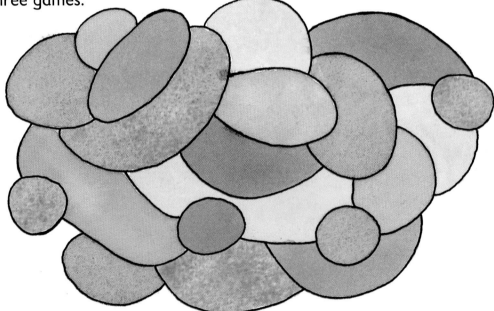

Challenge

Design your own game using the same rules.

A   Kim makes sausages by the metre.
Each metre has ten links of sausage.

0.7 m

Write the length of each of these strings of sausages in metres.

1.

2.

3.

4.

5.

6.

B   How many garlic sausages were made:
1. On Monday and Tuesday?
2. On Wednesday and Thursday?
3. By the end of the week?

How many veggi sausages were made:
4. On Tuesday and Wednesday?
5. On Thursday and Friday?
6. By the end of the week?

	Veggi sausage	Garlic sausage
Monday	2.4 m	3.8 m
Tuesday	4.6 m	5.9 m
Wednesday	3.1 m	7.2 m
Thursday	2.9 m	6.3 m
Friday	6.4 m	9.7 m

C   Find the totals of these sums.
1. 4.6 m + 2.4 m   2. 3.8 m + 3.6 m   3. 6.5 m + 3.8 m
4. 1.9 m + 7.6 m   5. 2.5 m + 7.5 m   6. 3.7 m + 2.6 m

D   Add these lengths.

1.	2.	3.	4.	5.
14.2 m	15.9 m	18.4 m	16.8 m	12.5 m
+ 12.6 m	+ 11.6 m	+ 17.7 m	+ 14.8 m	+ 13.9 m

Challenge

Write two lengths of sausages which make the following totals.
1. 8.6 m   2. 7.1 m   3. 5.1 m   4. 9.3 m   5. 7.0 m

Unit 6

Ribbons

 A Sunil takes 1.6 m of ribbon from each roll.
Write how much remains.

1. 5.0 m   2. 4.1 m   3. 3.5 m   4. 7.2 m   5. 4.3 m

B Look at the table.
Write how much of each
ribbon was sold.
  1. Embroidered
  2. Pink Silk
  3. Blue Silk
  4. Black Velvet
  5. Red Velvet

Ribbon	Start of day	End of day
Embroidered	14.2 m	8.6 m
Pink silk	12.0 m	5.8 m
Blue silk	10.5 m	7.9 m
Black velvet	8.7 m	2.8 m
Red velvet	6.3 m	4.5 m

C Answer these sums.
  1. 7.2 m − 4.6 m   2. 5.0 m − 3.2 m   3. 8.6 m − 4.7 m
  4. 6.4 m − 3.8 m   5. 5.1 m − 3.8 m   6. 7.5 m − 5.7 m

D Find the difference between each pair of lengths.

1. | 13.4 m | 18.2 m | 2. | 15.2 m | 13.7 m | 3. | 15.3 m | 11.9 m |

4. | 16.8 m | 18.2 m | 5. | 17.4 m | 20.0 m | 6. | 11.1 m | 10.6 m |

Challenge

These three lots of ribbon have a total length of 5.4 m.
The blue silk ribbon is 0.3 m shorter than the black velvet ribbon.
The blue silk ribbon is 0.3 m longer than the red velvet ribbon.
Find the length of each ribbon.

A Calculate the cost for each student.

1. ZIP

Gravity Boots

Control Key

Internet Card

2. ZORA

Computer Pad

Top

Action Belt

Power Pack

Gravity Boots	£7.50
Vision Helmet	£9.99
Control Key	£3.70
Computer Pad	£8.52
Internet Card	£3.60
Top	£8.65
Zimmer Socks	£2.45
Action Belt	£7.95
Back Pack	£5.65
Power Pack	£6.32

3. BAZ

Vision Helmet

Action Belt

Back Pack

Power Pack

4. NADA

Internet Card

Computer Pad

Zimmer Socks

Gravity Boots

Challenge

Which three of the items above cost £9.75?

B Find these totals.
1. £3.54 + £7.86
2. £7.44 + £5.68
3. £6.27 + £3.86
4. £9.26 + £8.71
5. £3.49 + £2.96
6. £4.18 + £6.77

C Here are the readings from Baz's power pack:

Write how many units he used on:
1. Monday and Tuesday
2. Wednesday and Thursday
3. Thursday and Friday
4. Monday, Tuesday and Wednesday
5. By the end of the week

	Units used
Monday	14.36
Tuesday	7.58
Wednesday	13.27
Thursday	15.95
Friday	22.14

A Find the difference in cost between the following computer games.

1. Snail Race and Rabbit Raid
2. Galactic Gerbils and Supernova
3. Super Tennis and Stellar Challenge
4. Snail Race and Super Tennis

£4.76   £5.84
£7.11   £6.28   £3.21
£8.97
£2.78
£7.35

 B Calculate the change from £10 for each of these:
1. Rabbit Raid
2. Football League
3. Alien Dynasty
4. Snail Race

 C Here are Sean's last two scores for each game.

	Score (thousand points)	
Football League	24.50	29.61
Super Tennis	14.26	16.71
Galactic Gerbils	12.35	18.59
Stellar Challenge	25.00	13.38
Rabbit Raid	19.63	13.59

Write the difference between his two scores for these games:
1. Football League
2. Super Tennis
3. Galactic Gerbils
4. Stellar Challenge
5. Rabbit Raid

 D Subtract these and write your answers.
1. $4.46 - 3.95$ 2. $8.24 - 3.65$ 3. $7.14 - 5.27$ 4. $6.94 - 1.86$
5. $5.21 - 2.99$ 6. $7.25 - 4.36$ 7. $5.28 - 1.74$ 8. $8.00 - 4.43$

Challenge

Sean, Kelly, Angelo and Melissa buy four games.
They want to share the cost equally.
Work out who must pay what to whom.
Write down your answer.

Sean spent £3
Kelly spent £2

Melissa spent £6
Angelo spent £5

A Copy and complete the tables of results for these number crunchers.

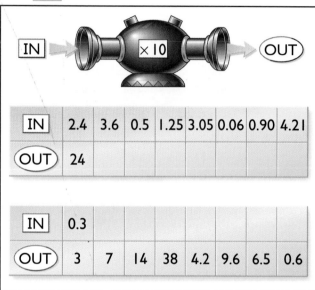

IN	2.4	3.6	0.5	1.25	3.05	0.06	0.90	4.21
OUT	24							

IN	0.3							
OUT	3	7	14	38	4.2	9.6	6.5	0.6

IN	123	206	158	42	7.2	4.5	1.6	0.
OUT	1.23							

IN	176							
OUT	1.76	4.65	3.7	5.8	0.42	0.214	0.335	0.02

B Write these lengths in centimetres.
1. 3.7 m   2. 5.6 m   3. 0.7 m   4. 1.2 m   5. 3.4 m   6. 2.9 m

C Write these lengths in metres.
1. 130 cm   2. 208 cm   3. 1526 cm
4. 5385 cm   5. 4205 cm   6. 68 cm

D Copy and complete these diagrams.

1.

2.

3.

A For each of these activities, start with 100 on a calculator.
You can only divide.

Find divisions that will produce
the following answers.

100

1.
0.1

2.
0.8

3.
2.5

4.
0.25

5.
0.16

6.
6.25

B Start with 100 again.
Now write the divisions that will produce these answers.

1.
9.090909

2.
1.5151515

3.
1.8181818

4.
3.030303

5.
4.5454545

6.
1.0101010

 ESTIGATE

Investigate divisions that will produce the following answers.

3.33333

2.22222

6.66666

Find some other divisions that produce repeating digits.

A A calculator changes a remainder into a decimal.

$17 \div 2 = 8$ r.1   On a calculator, $17 \div 2 =$ `8.5`

Write division sums to produce each of the following decimal remainders.

1. `0.625`   2. `0.75`   3. `0.25`   4. `0.4`   5. `0.125`

B Write the decimal remainders that are possible when you divide a whole number by these numbers.

1. 10   2. 5   3. 4   4. 8   5. 2

C Some divisions go on and on and on . . .

$$7 \overline{)20.000000000} \quad 2.857142857$$

Find out which of these divisions go on and on.

1. $7\overline{)94}$ 2. $5\overline{)47}$ 3. $9\overline{)68}$

4. $8\overline{)95}$ 5. $3\overline{)62}$ 6. $6\overline{)71}$

D Make a list of six divisions whose decimal remainders go on and on.

Challenge

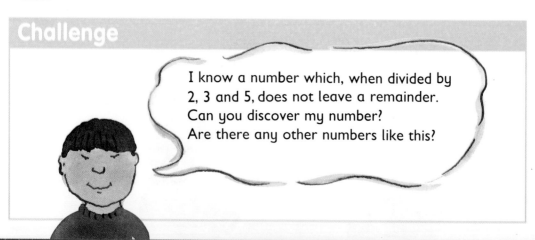

I know a number which, when divided by 2, 3 and 5, does not leave a remainder. Can you discover my number? Are there any other numbers like this?

Fractions into decimals

You can change fractions into decimals by dividing.

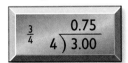 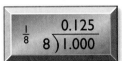

 Write the following fractions as decimals.

1. $\frac{1}{4}$ 2. $\frac{4}{5}$ 3. $\frac{3}{8}$ 4. $\frac{3}{5}$

5. $\frac{7}{8}$ 6. $\frac{5}{8}$ 7. $\frac{2}{5}$ 8. $\frac{7}{10}$

 Some fractions do not change into exact decimals.

Write these fractions as decimals.
Stop when you have six digits after the decimal.

1. $\frac{1}{3}$ 2. $\frac{4}{7}$ 3. $\frac{5}{9}$ 4. $\frac{5}{6}$ 5. $\frac{2}{9}$

 Play this game with a partner.
Each player draws a grid like this.

0							6

Take turns to roll two dice.
Divide one number by the other.
Write the answer on your grid in any space.
Numbers on the grid must always be in the correct
order, from lowest to highest.
Numbers cannot be used more than once.
If you cannot place your answer on the grid, miss that go.
See who is the first to finish their grid.

Decimal blanks

Write the digits 0–9 on small squares of paper.
Find a home for each digit.

 A Copy and complete these sums.
You will need to use each digit once.

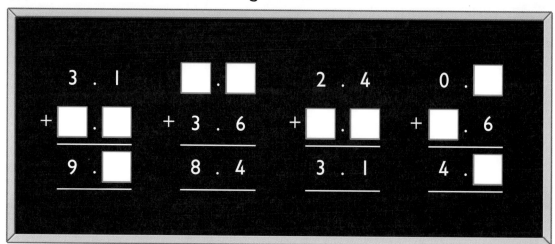

```
   3 . 1        □ . □       2 . 4        0 . □
 + □ . □      + 3 . 6     + □ . □      + □ . 6
 ─────────    ─────────   ─────────    ─────────
   9 . □        8 . 4       3 . 1        4 . □
```

B Now do the same with these sums.

```
   □ . 7        □ . □       □ . □        4 . □
 − 5 . 3      − 6 . □     − 1 . 8      − □ . 9
 ─────────    ─────────   ─────────    ─────────
   0 . □        2 . 9       1 . □        3 . 8
```

Challenge

Make up a similar set of sums for a friend to complete.

Unit 6  Animal magic

A Look at these flea jumps.
Answer the following questions.

1. How far would Francis go in two jumps?
2. How far did Freda and Felix jump altogether?
3. How much further did Flo jump than Frankie?
4. How much further must Francis jump to reach 3 m?
5. What is the difference between Felix's and Freda's jumps?

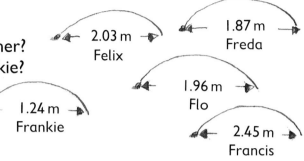

2.03 m
Felix

1.87 m
Freda

1.96 m
Flo

1.24 m
Frankie

2.45 m
Francis

B Look at these elephants.

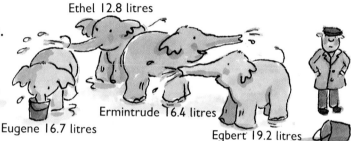

Ethel 12.8 litres

Edgar 17.5 litres

Enid 15.4 litres

Eugene 16.7 litres

Ermintrude 16.4 litres

Egbert 19.2 litres

Answer the following questions.

1. How much more water did Egbert squirt than Ethel?
2. How much did Edgar and Enid squirt altogether?
3. How much would Ermintrude squirt in two goes?
4. What was the difference between Eugene's and Ethel's squirts?
5. Who squirted most, Enid and Edgar or Ermintrude and Eugene?

C Look at these monkeys.

Manny 4.12 kg

Mona 2.71 kg

Monty 2.45 kg   Mia 3.25 kg

Milo 3.02 kg

Answer the following questions.

1. What is the total weight that Monty and Mia are carrying?
2. What is the total weight that Mona, Manny and Milo are carrying?
3. How much more is Manny carrying than Mia?
4. What is the difference between the weights that Monty and Mona are carrying?
5. Which two are carrying a total of 5.96 kg?

The sign % means 'per cent'.
Per cent means 'out of a hundred'.
40% means 40 out of 100.

A Write these as percentages.

1. 50 out of 100

2. 70 out of 100

3. 90 out of 100

4. 60 out of 100

5. 10 out of 100

6. 80 out of 100

B Write what percentage of bugs have:

1. Red backs
2. One pair of wings
3. Two pairs of wings
4. Yellow stripes
5. Six legs
6. Eight legs
7. No wings

Write these percentages as fractions. $20\% = \frac{20}{100}$

C
1. 40%
2. 10%
3. 60%
4. 50%
5. 80%
6. 90%
7. 30%
8. 70%

Percentages

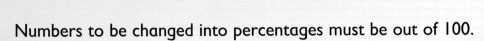

Numbers to be changed into percentages must be out of 100.

$$\frac{3}{10} = \frac{30}{100} = 30\%$$ $$\frac{25}{50} = \frac{50}{100} = 50\%$$

A Write these fractions as percentages.

1. $\frac{7}{10}$ 2. $\frac{3}{20}$ 3. $\frac{30}{50}$ 4. $\frac{45}{50}$

5. $\frac{17}{20}$ 6. $\frac{15}{50}$ 7. $\frac{8}{10}$ 8. $\frac{3}{10}$

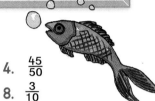

B Write what percentage of fish are:

1. red;
2. blue;
3. yellow;
4. yellow and red;
5. yellow and black;
6. blue and red.

C Write the percentage of each shape which is coloured red.

1.   2.   3.   4.

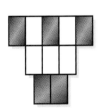

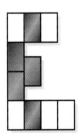

D Draw four shapes like this.
Colour 50% of each shape.
Make each shape a different pattern.

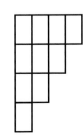

Skaters' chase

Play this game with a partner.
Put a red counter on the red spot.
Put a blue counter on the blue spot.

Rules

Take turns to move from square to square.
The red skater moves first and tries to catch the blue skater.
A move is along any line to the next square.
Squares may not be visited more than once.
The red skater must catch the blue skater in seven moves or less.

Star puzzle

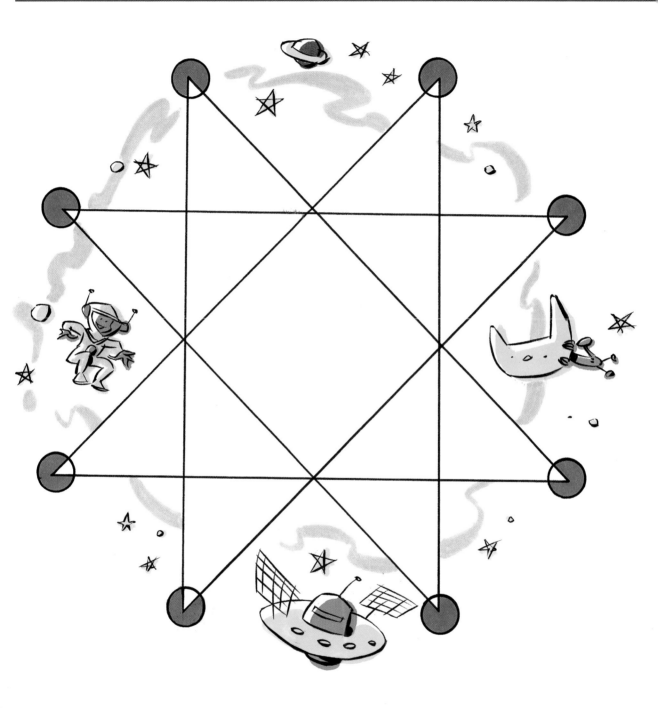

Put a counter on any unoccupied spot.
Move it along a straight line to another unoccupied spot.
Do this as many times as you can.
Can you end up with seven counters on the star?
Write down your solution to the puzzle.

Information

Multiplication square

×	1	2	3	4	5	6	7	8	9	10
1	1	2	3	4	5	6	7	8	9	10
2	2	4	6	8	10	12	14	16	18	20
3	3	6	9	12	15	18	21	24	27	30
4	4	8	12	16	20	24	28	32	36	40
5	5	10	15	20	25	30	35	40	45	50
6	6	12	18	24	30	36	42	48	54	60
7	7	14	21	28	35	42	49	56	63	70
8	8	16	24	32	40	48	56	64	72	80
9	9	18	27	36	45	54	63	72	81	90
10	10	20	30	40	50	60	70	80	90	100

Square and triangle numbers to 100

Square numbers	1	4	9	16	25	36	49	64	81	100			
Triangle numbers	1	3	6	10	15	21	28	36	45	55	66	78	91

Measurements

10 mm = 1 cm
100 cm = 1 m
1000 mm = 1 m
1000 m = 1 km

1000 g = 1 kg
1000 kg = 1 tonne

10 ml = 1 cl
100 cl = 1 l
1000 ml = 1 l